ANTI-INFLAMMATORY

50 Recipes That Will Help You Unravel the Secrets of This New Way of Understanding Alimentation.

Soothing Cooking

Table of Contents

INTRODUCTION

The Anti-Inflammatory Diet

If you have a condition that causes inflammation, such as chronic peptic, ulcer, asthma, tuberculosis, sinusitis, rheumatoid periodontitis, Crohn's disease, active hepatitis, or arthritis, an anti-inflammatory diet can help. The connection between inflammation and heart disease, arthritis, and other chronic ailments is becoming increasingly clear. Many food allergies and poor dietary choices over stimulate the immune system and cause inflammatory responses that destroy the body's wellness and pave the way for ill health. Inflammation can undermine the overall health of the body, leading to disease down the road and impairing the proper functioning of the brain, joints, cardiovascular system, and skin.

As you will see, the anti-inflammatory diet is simple to follow and is not overly strict. You are able to adjust the diet according to your own preferences. Nevertheless, there are some cons that you should know. The anti-inflammatory diet can be costly as it is recommended that you eat organic food. Likewise, the diet contains a number of allergens, such as nuts, seeds, and soy.

However, eating the right adjusted food will help to eliminate the cons of the diet. It is highly recommended to consult your doctor for a complete medical examination before starting. By doing this, you can avoid unwanted effects of diet.

Ways of Reducing Inflammation Overnight

- Eat salads every day.
- Keep your blood sugar in normal parameters by taking balanced snacks without added sugar and refined carbs.
- Sleep for 7-8 hours every night.
- Take a break from alcohol and add green tea to your routine instead of tea or coffee.
- Go for walk every daily.
- Cut out added sugars and trans fats from your diet and focus on choosing primarily whole and minimally processed foods.

Anti-Inflammatory Foods

1. Fruits
2. Vegetables
3. Legumes
4. Beans
5. Lentils
6. Whole Grains
7. Fish
8. Olive Oil
9. Poultry
10. Nuts
11. Low-Fat Dairy
12. Seeds

It's believed that the antioxidants in brightly colored fruits and vegetables may lessen the effect of free radicals, which damage cells. So try to incorporate more green vegetables and fruits into your diet. To fight inflammation, go for whole, unprocessed foods with no added sugar.

Worst Food for Inflammation

- Processed meat
- Refined sugar
- Alcohol
- Vegetable oils
- Processed fruits
- Saturated fats
- Gluten
- Artificial trans fats
- Artificial preservatives
- White bread
- Cereals
- White pasta
- Juices
- Sodas
- cookies
- Ice cream
- Candies
- Processed and cured meat

You should stay away from ultra-processed foods, like microwaveable dinners, hot dogs, processed meats, dehydrated soups, chicken nuggets, sugary cereals, biscuits, baked goods, and sauces. These foods have little nutritional value and are high in salt, added sugars, and saturated fat. All of these ingredients are associated with promoting inflammation in the body.

Anti-Inflammatory Diet Tips

- You should gradually replace fast food meals with healthful, homemade lunches.
- Replace sodas and other sugary beverages with still or sparkling mineral water
- Take a variety of fruits, vegetables, and healthy snacks.
- Maintain and control your blood sugar levels by avoiding white foods such as sugar, salt, etc.
- Eat food that is rich in probiotics every day. This will improve the gut's microbe barrier. Such foods are fermented vegetables/fruits, miso, sauerkraut, yogurt, kombucha, kimchi, and milk.
- Sleep for 7 to 8 hours.
- For faster treatment, drink antioxidant beverages. Chili pepper thyme, oregano, basil, and curcumin have anti-inflammatory features and serve as natural painkillers.
- Balance your mind by practicing yoga, meditation or biofeedback.
- Make yourself feel healthier by exercising daily.
- Increase the use of green tea instead of coffee and black tea.

Anti-Inflammation Diet Meal Plan for 1 Week

<u>Monday</u>

Breakfast

Steel cut oats with blueberries

Lunch

Mexican chopped salad with creamy avocado dressing

Pineapple ginger smoothie

Dinner

Thai vegetable curry fry

<u>Tuesday</u>

Breakfast

Steel cut oats with blueberries

Lunch

Sautéed mushroom, kale, and egg seasoned with turmeric.

Pineapple ginger smoothie.

Dinner

Salmon cake

Broccoli and green salad

Wednesday

Breakfast

Millet porridge cooked in coconut milk with mango and blueberries.

Lunch

Large salad topped with left over salmon cakes and a balsamic dressing.

Pineapple ginger smoothie

Dinner

Vegetable burger

Baked sweet potatoes

Thursday

Breakfast

Millet porridge cooked in coconut milk with mango and blueberries.

Lunch

Loaded baked sweet potato

Spiced banana almond smoothie

Dinner

Grilled chicken with sautéed spinach

Friday

Breakfast

Cooked quinoa topped with raspberries and toasted walnuts.

Lunch

Large mixed salad with sunny side up egg

Spiced banana almond smoothie

Dinner

Spring barley and quinoa risotto with asparagus and shitake mushrooms

Saturday

Breakfast

Cooked quinoa topped with raspberries and toasted walnuts

Lunch

Lentil vegetable bowl

Dinner

Grilled salmon

Asparagus

Potato

Sunday

Breakfast

Sweet potato pancake with almond butter

Lunch

Lentil vegetable bowl

Dinner

Quinoa stuffed peppers

BREAKFAST

Healthy Yam Cakes

Servings: 12

Preparation Time: 20 Minutes

Per Servings: 219 calories,7.1g protein, 18.4g carbohydrates, 13.3g fat, 4.1g fiber, 55mg cholesterol, 241mg sodium, 286mg potassium.

Ingredients:

- 2 Cups almond flour
- 2 Oz brown rice, cooked
- 2 Tablespoons flax meal
- 2 Teaspoons baking soda
- 4 Eggs, beaten
- 2 Small yellow onions chopped
- 2 Teaspoons cayenne pepper
- 2 Teaspoons olive oil
- 14 Oz yams, peeled, grated

Procedure:

13. First, mix yams with almond flour, brown rice, flax meal, baking soda, eggs, onion, and cayenne pepper.

14. Now, make medium-size cakes.

15. Line the baking tray with baking paper.

16. Then, put the yam cakes inside and sprinkle them with olive oil.

17. Finally, bake the yam cakes at 400F for 10 minutes

Healthy Pistachios Salad

Servings: 4

Preparation Time: 15 minutes

Per Serving:: 264 calories,7.8g protein, 19.6g carbohydrates, 20.7g fat, 5.1g fiber, 0mg cholesterol, 161mg sodium, 763mg potassium.

Ingredients

- 1 Cup tomatoes, chopped
- 2 Cucumbers, chopped
- 2 Sweet peppers chopped
- 1 Cup fresh cilantro, chopped
- 4 Oz pistachios, chopped
- 2 Tablespoons lemon juice
- 2 Tablespoons olive oil

Procedure:

1. First, put all ingredients in the salad bowl.
2. Then, gently shake the salad.

Homemade Zucchini Eggs

Servings: 4

Preparation Time: 30 Minutes

Per Serving: 162 calories, 8.5g protein, 6.2g carbohydrates, 12g fat, 1.3g fiber, 166mg cholesterol, 93mg sodium, 393mg potassium.

Ingredients:

- 2 Zucchinis spiralized
- 2 Tablespoons olive oil
- 2 Teaspoons dried rosemary
- 1 Cup plain yogurt
- 4 Eggs, beaten

Procedure:

1. First, preheat the olive oil in the skillet.
2. Then, add eggs and top them with dried rosemary.
3. Now, cook the eggs for 3 minutes on low heat.
4. After this, add zucchini and plain yogurt.
5. Finally, mix the mixture gently, close the lid, and cook it on low heat for 12 minutes.

Easy Pears and Cherries

Servings: 8

Preparation Time: 10 minutes

Per Serving: calories 211, fat 16.9, fiber 3.4, carbs 15.8, protein 2.8

Ingredients:

- 2 Cups almond milk
- 2 Cups pears, cored and cubed
- 2 Cups cherries, pitted and halved
- 1 Teaspoon vanilla extract
- 4 Tablespoons cocoa powder
- 4 Tablespoons walnuts, chopped

Procedure:

1. Now, take a bowl, mix the pears with the cherries and the other ingredients, toss, divide into smaller bowls and serve for breakfast.

Quick Turmeric Cucumber and Mango Salad

Servings: 4

Preparation Time: 10 Minutes

Per Serving: calories 68, fat 0.5, fiber 2, carbs 17.1, protein 1.3

Ingredients:

- 2 Cups mango, peeled and cubed
- 2 Cups cucumber, peeled and cubed
- 1 Cup lime juice
- 2 Teaspoons ginger powder
- 1 Teaspoon turmeric powder
- 2 Teaspoons mint, dried
- 2 Teaspoons chia seeds
- 2 Teaspoons chives, chopped

Procedure

1. Now, take a bowl, combine the mango with the cucumber, the lime juice and the other ingredients, toss, divide into smaller bowls and serve for breakfast.

Homemade Mango Ginger Smoothie

Servings: 4

Preparation Time: 10 Minutes

Per Serving: calories 519, fat 30.5, fiber 8.6, carbs 66.1, protein 5.8

Ingredients:

- 2 Cups almond milk
- 4 Mangoes, peeled and cubed
- 2 Tablespoons ginger, grated
- 1 Cup water
- 2 Tablespoons nutmeg, ground
- 2 Tablespoons maple syrup

Procedure:

1. Firstly, in your blender, combine the mangoes with the milk and the other ingredients, pulse well, divide into glasses and serve for breakfast.

Quick Eggs with Herbs

Servings: 8

Preparation Time: 25 Minutes

Per Serving: calories 200, fat 15.9, fiber 1, carbs 3.9, protein 11.5

Ingredients:

- 4 Tablespoons olive oil
- 2 Yellow onions, chopped
- 16 Eggs, whisked
- A pinch of salt and black pepper
- 2 Tablespoons coriander, ground
- 2 Tablespoons chives, chopped
- 2 Tablespoons rosemary, chopped
- 2 Tablespoons cilantro, chopped
- 2 Tablespoons parsley, chopped

Procedure:

1. First, heat up a pan with the oil over medium heat, add the onion, stir and sauté for 3 minutes.

2. Now, add the eggs and the other ingredients, toss, cook for 12 minutes more, divide into bowls and serve for breakfast.

Easy Portuguese Salad

Servings: 8

Preparation Time: 10 Minutes

Per Serving: 107 calories,1.8g protein, 10.5g carbohydrates, 7.4g fat, 2.9g fiber, 0mg cholesterol, 9mg sodium, 405mg potassium.

Ingredients:

- 6 Cups tomatoes, sliced
- 4 Red onions, peeled, sliced
- 4 Tablespoons olive oil
- 1 Teaspoon cayenne pepper

Procedure:

1. First, mix tomatoes with red onions and cayenne pepper.
2. Then, top the salad with olive oil and stir it before serving.

Homemade Chia Coconut and Walnut Porridge

Servings: 8

Preparation Time: 10 Minutes

Per Serving: calories 647, fat 58.8, fiber 13.4, carbs 26.4, protein 14.3

Ingredients:

- 2 Cups walnuts, chopped and toasted
- 6 Tablespoons chia seeds
- 4 Cups almond milk
- 1 Cup coconut, shredded and toasted
- 2 Bananas peeled and mashed
- 2 Tablespoons coconut oil, melted
- 1 Teaspoon turmeric powder

Procedure:

1. Now, heat up a pot with the milk over medium heat, add the chia seeds, the walnuts and the other ingredients, toss, simmer for 5 minutes, divide into bowls and serve warm for breakfast.

Easy Mushrooms Frittata

Servings: 8

Preparation Time: 40 Minutes

Per Serving: calories 200, fat 3, fiber 6, carbs 14, protein 6

Ingredients:

- 1 Cup coconut milk, unsweetened
- 12 Eggs
- 2 Yellow onions, chopped
- 8 Ounces white mushrooms, sliced
- 4 Tablespoons olive oil
- 4 Tablespoons baby spinach
- A pinch of salt and black pepper

Procedure

1. First, heat up a pan with the oil over medium-high heat, add the onion, stir and cook for 2-3 minutes.
2. Then, take a bowl, mix the eggs with salt and pepper, stir well and pour over the mushrooms.

3. Finally, add the spinach, mix a bit, place in the oven and bake at 360 degrees F for 25 minutes. Slice the frittata and serve it for breakfast.

Quick Almond Breakfast Crepes

Servings: 8

Preparation Time: 20 Minutes

Per Serving: calories 121, fat 3, fiber 6, carbs 14, protein 6

Ingredients:

- 4 Eggs
- 2 Teaspoons vanilla extract
- 1 Cup almond milk, unsweetened
- 1 Cup water
- 4 Tablespoons agave nectar
- 2 Cups coconut flour
- 6 Tablespoons coconut oil, melted

Procedure:

1. First, take a bowl whisk the eggs with the vanilla extract, almond milk water and agave nectar.
2. Then, add the flour and 2 tablespoons oil gradually and stir until you obtain a smooth batter.
3. Finally, heat up a pan with the rest of the oil over medium heat, add some of the batters, spread it into

the pan and cook the crepe until it's golden on both sides, then transfer to a plate. Repeat with the rest of the batter and serve the crepes for breakfast.

Quick Millet Muffins

Servings: 24

Preparation Time: 30 Minutes

Per Serving: calories 167, fat 4, fiber 7, carbs 15, protein 6

Ingredients:

- 1 Cup coconut oil, melted
- 2 Eggs
- 1 Teaspoon vanilla extract
- 2 Teaspoons baking powder
- 3 Cups organic millet, cooked
- 1 Cup coconut sugar
- Cooking spray

Procedure:

1. First, in a blender, blend the melted coconut oil with the egg, vanilla extract, baking powder, millet and sugar. Grease a muffin tray with cooking spray and divide the millet mix into each cup.
2. Then, place the muffins in the oven and bake at 350 degrees F for 30 minutes.

3. Finally, let the muffins cool and then serve!

Healthy Cocoa Buckwheat Granola

Servings: 12

Preparation Time: 55 Minutes

Per Serving: calories 161, fat 3, fiber 5, carbs 11; protein

Ingredients:

- 4 Cups oats
- 2 Cups buckwheat
- 2 Cups sunflower seeds
- 2 Cups pumpkin seeds
- 3 Cups dates, pitted and chopped
- 2 Cups apple puree
- 12 Tablespoons coconut oil
- 10 Tablespoons cocoa powder
- 2 Teaspoons fresh grated ginger

Procedure:

1. Firstly, in a large bowl, mix the oats with the buckwheat, sunflower seeds, pumpkin seeds, dates, apple puree, oil, cocoa powder, and ginger, then stir really well.

2. Then, line the baking sheet, press well and place in the oven at 360 degrees F for 45 minutes. Leave the granola to cool down, slice and serve for breakfast.

LUNCH

Homemade Mint Chicken

Servings: 8

Preparation Time: 40 Minutes

Per Serving: 434 calories, 65.7g protein, 0.6g carbohydrates, 16.9g fat, 0.3g fiber, 202mg cholesterol, 196mg sodium, 572mg potassium

Ingredients:

- 4 Pounds chicken fillet, chopped
- 2 Tablespoons mint, chopped
- 2 Tablespoons ground black pepper
- 1 Tablespoon turmeric
- 1 Cup of water

Procedure:

1. First, mix chicken fillet with mint, ground black pepper, and ground turmeric.
2. Then, put the chicken in the baking pan, add water, and bake it at 365F for 30 minutes.

Easy Salmon with Black Beans

Servings: 8

Preparation Time: 35 Minutes

Per Serving: calories 219, fat 8, fiber 8, carbs 12, protein 8

Ingredients:

- 2 Cupscanned black beans, drained and rinsed
- 8 Garlic cloves, minced
- 2 Yellow onions chopped
- 2 Tablespoons olive oil
- 8 Salmons fillets, boneless
- 1 Teaspoon coriander, ground
- 2 Teaspoons turmeric powder
- 4 Tomatoes, cubed
- 1 Cup chicken stock
- A pinch of salt and black pepper
- 1 Teaspoon cumin seeds
- 2 Teaspoons chives, chopped

Procedure:

1. First, heat up a pan with the oil over medium heat, add the onion and the garlic and sauté for 5 minutes.
2. Then, add the fish and sear it for 2 minutes on each side.
3. Finally, add the beans and the other ingredients, toss gently and cook for 10 minutes more.
4. Now, divide the mix between plates and serve right away for lunch

Homemade Chicken Chilli with Tomatoes

Servings: 12

Preparation Time: 45 Minutes

Per Serving: calories 300, fat 2, fiber 10, carbs 15, protein 11

Ingredients:

- 2 Yellow onions chopped
- 4 Tablespoons olive oil
- 4 Garlic cloves, minced
- 2 Pounds chicken breast, skinless, boneless and cubed
- 2 Green bell peppers, chopped
- 4 Cups chicken stock
- 2 Tablespoons cocoa powder
- 4 Tablespoons chili powder
- 2 Teaspoons smoked paprika
- 2 Cups canned tomatoes, chopped
- 2 Tablespoons cilantro, chopped
- A pinch of salt and black pepper

Procedure:

1. Firstly, heat up a pot with the oil over medium heat, add the onion and the garlic and sauté for 5 minutes.
2. Then, add the meat and brown it for 5 minutes more.
3. In conclusion, add the rest of the ingredients, toss, cook over medium heat for 40 minutes.
4. Now, divide the chili into bowls and serve for lunch.

Easy Veggie Cabbage Soup

Servings: 12

Preparation Time: 45 Minutes

Per Serving: calories 212, fat 5, fiber 7, carbs 14, protein 12

Ingredients:

- 2 Yellows onions chopped
- 2 Green cabbages head, shredded
- 4 Tablespoons olive oil
- 10 Cups veggie stock
- 2 Carrots, peeled and grated
- A pinch of salt and black pepper
- 2 Tablespoons cilantro, chopped
- 4 Teaspoons thyme, chopped
- 1 Teaspoon smoked paprika
- 1 Teaspoon hot paprika
- 2 Tablespoons lemon juice

Procedure:

1. Firstly, heat up a pot with the oil over medium heat, add the onion and the carrot and sauté for 5 minutes.
2. Then, add the cabbage and the other ingredients, toss, simmer over medium heat for 30 minutes

Quick Sweet Chicken Bake

Servings: 4

Preparation Time: 40 Minutes

Per Serving: 237 calories, 33.3g protein, 4.8g carbohydrates, 8.8g fat, 1.1g fiber, 101mg cholesterol, 100mg sodium, 365mg potassium

Ingredients:

- 2 Pounds chicken fillet, chopped
- 2 Cups peaches, chopped
- 1 Cup of water
- 2 Teaspoons ground nutmeg
- 2 Teaspoons ground clove
- 1 Lemon, chopped

Procedure:

1. Firstly, mix the chicken fillet with ground nutmeg and ground clove.
2. Then, the chicken in the baking pan.
3. Finally, water, lemon, and peaches.

4. Now, close the lid and cook the meal in the oven at 365F for 30 minutes.

Delicious Cod Stew with Cauliflower

Servings: 8

Preparation Time: 35 Minutes

Per Serving: calories 281, fat 6, fiber 4, carbs 8, protein 12

Ingredients:

- 1 Pound cauliflower florets
- 2 Pounds cod fillets, boneless, skinless and cubed
- 2 Tablespoons cry olive oil
- 2 Yellow onions chopped
- 1 Teaspoon cumin seeds
- 2 Green chilis, chopped
- 1 Teaspoon turmeric powder
- 4 Tomatoes chopped
- A pinch of salt and black pepper
- 1 Cup chicken stock
- 2 Tablespoons cilantro, chopped

Procedure:

1. Firstly, heat up a pot with the oil over medium heat, add the onion, chili, cumin and turmeric, stir and cook for 5 minutes.
2. Then, add the cauliflower, the fish and the other ingredients, toss, bring to a simmer and cook over medium heat for 25 minutes more.
3. Now, divide the stew into bowls and serve.

Easy Cocoa Buckwheat Granola

Servings: 12

Preparation Time: 55 Minutes

Per Serving: calories 161, fat 3, fiber 5, carbs 11, protein 7

Ingredients:

- 4 Cups oats
- 2 Cups buckwheat
- 2 Cups sunflower seeds
- 2 Cups pumpkin seeds
- 3 Cupsdates, pitted and chopped
- 2 Cups apple puree
- 12 Tablespoons coconut oil
- 10 Tablespoons cocoa powder
- 2 Teaspoons fresh grated ginger

Directions:

1. Firstly, in a large bowl, mix the oats with the buckwheat, sunflower seeds, pumpkin seeds, dates, apple puree, oil, cocoa powder, and ginger, then stir really well.

2. Then, spread on a lined baking sheet, press well and place in the oven at 360 degrees F for 45 minutes.
3. Finally, leave the granola to cool down, slice and serve for breakfast.

Homemade Mushroom Frittata

Servings: 4

Preparation Time: 40 Minutes

Per Serving: calories 200, fat 3, fiber 6, carbs 14, protein 6

Ingredients:

- 1 Cup coconut milk, unsweetened
- 12 Eggs
- 2 Yellow onions, chopped
- 8 Ounces white mushrooms, sliced
- 4 Tablespoons olive oil
- 4 Cups baby spinach
- A pinch of salt and black pepper

Procedure:

1. First, heat up a pan with the oil over medium-high heat, add the onion, stir and cook for 2-3 minutes.
2. Then, add the mushrooms, salt and pepper, stir and cook for 2 minutes more. In a bowl, mix the eggs with salt and pepper, stir well and pour over the mushrooms

3. . Finally, add the spinach, mix a bit, place in the oven and bake at 360 degrees F for 25 minutes. Slice the frittata and serve it for breakfast.

Easy Almonds Breakfast Crepes

Servings: 8

Preparation Time: 20 Minutes

Per Serving: calories 121, fat 3, fiber 6, carbs 14, protein 6

Ingredients:

- 4 Eggs
- 2 Cups vanilla extract
- 1 Cup almond milk, unsweetened
- 1 Cup water
- 4 Tablespoons agave nectar
- 2 Cups coconut flour
- 6 Tablespoons coconut oil, melted

Procedure:

1. Firstly, in a bowl, whisk the eggs with the vanilla extract, almond milk, water and agave nectar.
2. Then, the flour and 2 tablespoons oil gradually and stir until you obtain a smooth batter.
3. In conclusion, heat up a pan with the rest of the oil over medium heat, add some of the batter, spread into the

pan and cook the crepe until it's golden on both sides, then transfer to a plate. Repeat with the rest of the batter and serve the crepes for breakfast.

Quick Tomato Chicken

Servings: 8

Preparation Time: 35 Minutes

Per Serving: 274 calories, 34g protein, 6.4g carbohydrates, 12.1g fat, 1.7g fiber, 101mg cholesterol, 103mg sodium, 534mg potassium

Ingredients:

- 2 Onions, diced
- 4 Cups tomatoes, chopped
- 2 chilli peppers, chopped
- 2 Garlic clove, chopped
- 2 Tablespoons olive oil
- 2 Pounds chicken fillet, chopped

Procedure:

1. First, all ingredients in the saucepan and carefully mix.
2. Then, the lid and cook the chicken for 25 minutes on medium heat.
3. Now, stir the chicken from time to time to avoid burning.

Healthy Green Beans and Carrot Soup

Servings: 12

Preparation Time: 45 Minutes

Per Serving: calories 224, fat 2, fiber 12, carbs 10, protein 17

Ingredients:

- 2 Yellow onions chopped
- 2 Pounds green beans, trimmed and halved
- 2 Carrots, peeled and grated
- 4 Tomatoes cubed
- 2 Tablespoons olive oil
- 4 Teaspoons cumin, ground
- 12 Cups veggie stock
- 1 Teaspoon chipotle chili powder
- 2 Teaspoons cilantro, chopped

Procedure:

1. Firstly, heat up a pot with the oil over medium heat, add the onion and the carrot and sauté for 5 minutes.

2. Then, add the green beans and the rest of the ingredients, toss, bring to a simmer and cook over medium heat for 30 minutes.
3. Now, ladle the soup into bowls and serve.

Quick Millet Muffins

Servings: 24

Preparation Time: 25 Minutes

Per Serving: calories 167, fat 4, fiber 7, carbs 15, protein 6

Ingredients:

- 1 Cup coconut oil, melted
- 2 Eggs
- 1 Teaspoon vanilla extract
- 2 Teaspoons baking powder
- 3 Cups organic millet, cooked
- 1 Cup coconut sugar
- Cooking spray

Procedure:

1. Firstly, in a blender, blend the melted coconut oil with the egg, vanilla extract, baking powder, millet and sugar.
2. Then, grease a muffin tray with cooking spray and divide the millet mix into each cup.

3. Finally, place the muffins in the oven and bake at 350 degrees F for 30 minutes. Let the muffins cool and then serve!

Homemade Honey Duck Fillet

Servings: 8

Preparation Time: 25 Minutes

Per Serving: 189 calories, 33.5g protein, 4.7g carbohydrates, 4.2g fat, 0.2g fiber, 0mg cholesterol, 171mg sodium, 89mg potassium

Ingredients:

- 2 Pounds duck fillet, chopped
- 2 Tablespoons raw honey
- 2 Teaspoons ground turmeric
- 1 Teaspoon dried mint
- 2 Tablespoons olive oil

Procedure:

1. First, mix duck fillet with dried mint and ground turmeric.
2. Then, preheat the olive oil and put the duck pieces inside.
3. Finally, roasted them for 10 minutes. Stir the meat from time to time.

4. After this, add honey and carefully mix the meal.

5. Now, close the lid and cook it for 5 minutes more.

DINNER

Delicious Mint Green Beans

Servings: 8

Preparation Time: 30 Minutes

Per Serving: 65 calories, 2.1g protein, 8.2g carbohydrates, 3.6g fat, 3.9g fiber, 0mg cholesterol, 7mg sodium, 240mg potassium

Ingredients:

- 2 Pounds green beans, trimmed, chopped
- 2 Teaspoons dried mint
- 2 Tablespoons olive oil
- 2 Tablespoons chili flakes

Procedure:

1. First, put the green beans in the mixing bowl.
2. Then, add dried mint, olive oil, and chili flakes. Shake the mixture well.
3. Now, transfer it to the baking tray and bake at 365F for 20 minutes.

Quick Carrot Noodles

Servings: 12

Preparation Time: 15 Minutes

Per Serving: 45 calories, 0.5g protein, 6g carbohydrates, 2.3g fat, 1.5g fiber, 0mg cholesterol, 42mg sodium, 196mg potassium

Ingredients:

- 12 Carrots, spiralized
- 2 Tablespoons olive oil
- 2 Teaspoons dried cilantro
- 1 Teaspoon dried rosemary

Procedure:

1. First, take the bowl, mix carrots with olive oil, dried cilantro, and rosemary.
2. Now, carefully mix the meal and leave for 5-7 minutes to marinate.

Delicious Pork with Pineapple Mix

Servings: 8

Preparation Time: 50 Minutes

Per Serving: calories 250, fat 5, fiber 6, carbs 8, protein 17

Ingredients:

- 8 Pork chops
- 4 Tablespoons olive oil
- 1 Cup vegetable stock
- 8 Scallions, chopped
- 2 Cups pineapple, peeled and cubed
- 2 Mangoes, peeled and cubed
- 8 Tablespoons lime juice
- 2 Handful basils, chopped
- A pinch of salt and cayenne pepper

Procedure:

1. First, heat up a pan with the oil over medium heat, add the scallions and the meat and brown for 5 minutes.

2. Then, add the pineapple and the other ingredients, toss, cook over medium heat for 35 minutes more, divide between plates and serve.

Easy Orange shrimp Mix

Servings: 8

Preparation Time: 15 Minutes

Per Serving: calories 230, fat 6.2, fiber 5, carbs 8, protein 4

Ingredients:

- 2 Pounds shrimp, peeled and deveined
- 2 Tablespoons lemon juice
- 1 Teaspoon sweet paprika
- 4 Tablespoons olive oil
- 2 Teaspoons saffron powder
- 2 Teaspoons coriander , ground
- 2 Teaspoons orange zest, grated
- 1 Teaspoon cloves, ground
- 2 Tablespoons cilantro, chopped

Procedure:

1. First, heat up a pan with the oil over medium heat, add the shrimp, lemon juice, saffron and the other ingredients, toss, cook for 8 minutes,
2. Now, divide the mix into bowls and serve.

Quickly Lemon Chicken Mix

Servings: 8

Preparation Time: 40 Minutes

Per Serving: calories 288, fat 6, fiber 5, carbs 14, protein 20

Ingredients:

- 2 Tablespoons lemon zest
- 4 Tablespoons lemon juice
- 2 Tablespoons chopped thyme
- 3 Tablespoons Greek seasoning
- 10 Tablespoons olive oil
- 6 Garlic cloves, minced
- 8 Chicken breasts, skinless and boneless
- 2 Cups rice, cooked
- 1 Cup veggie stock
- 2 Cups grape tomatoes, halved
- 4 Small cucumbers, sliced
- 6 Scallions, chopped
- 2 Cups chopped parsley
- 1 Cup chopped mint

Procedure:

1. Firstly, in a baking dish, mix the chicken with the lemon zest, half of the lemon juice, thyme, garlic, Greek seasoning, stock and 2 tablespoons oil.
2. Then, put the seasonings into the chicken well, then bake in the oven at 400 degrees F for 30 minutes. Once cooked, divide between plates.
3. Finally, in a bowl, mix the rice with the rest of the lemon juice, tomatoes, cucumbers, scallions, parsley, mint, salt, and pepper, then toss and add next to the chicken and serve.

Delicious Marinated Collard Greens

Servings: 8

Preparation Time: 20 Minutes

Per Serving: 84 calories, 1.7g protein, 4.5g carbohydrates, 7.6g fat, 2.4g fiber, 0mg cholesterol, 14mg sodium, 20mg potassium

Ingredients:

- 20 Oz collard greens, chopped
- 6 Tablespoons lemon juice
- 2 Tablespoons minced garlic
- 1 Teaspoon minced ginger
- 4 Tablespoons olive oil

Procedure:

1. First, in the mixing bowl, mix lemon juice with minced garlic, minced ginger, and olive oil.
2. Then, add collard greens and carefully mix the mixture.
3. Now, leave the meal for 10 minutes to marinate.

Healthy Eggplants Ring

Servings: 8

Preparation Time: 25 Minutes

Per Serving: 150 calories, 5.2g protein, 26.6g carbohydrates, 4.5g fat, 14.6g fiber, 1mg cholesterol, 20mg sodium, 994mg potassium

Ingredients:

- 6 Egg plants , sliced
- 4 Tablespoons minced garlic
- 1 Cup plain yogurt
- 2 Teaspoons olive oil

Procedure:

1. Firstly, preheat the skillet well.
2. Then, add olive oil.
3. In conclusion, the sliced eggplants in the skillet in one layer and roast them for 2 minutes per side.
4. Then, mix plain yogurt with minced garlic.
5. Now, top the eggplants with a plain yogurt mixture.

Easy Chicken with Mushrooms and Cilantro

Servings: 8

Preparation Time: 50 Minutes

Per Serving: calories 210, fat 5, fiber 8, carbs 15, protein 11

Ingredients:

- 2 Yellows onions, chopped
- 2 Pounds chickens breast, skinless, boneless and roughly cubed
- 4 Tablespoons olive oil
- 2 Cups white mushrooms, sliced
- 2 Teaspoons turmeric powder
- 2 Cups chicken stock
- 4 Garlic cloves, minced
- 4 Teaspoons rosemary, chopped
- Salt and black pepper to the tastes
- 2 Tablespoons balsamic vinegar
- 2 Tablespoons cilantro, chopped

Procedure:

1. First, heat up a pan with the oil over medium heat, add the onion and the mushrooms and sauté for 10 minutes.
2. Then, add the meat and brown for 5 minutes more.
3. Now, add the garlic and the other ingredients, toss, cook over medium heat for 25 minutes more, divide between plates and serve.

Quickly Rosemary Salmon with Fennel

Servings: 8

Preparation Time: 20 Minutes

Per Serving: calories 200, fat 2, fiber 4, carbs 10, protein 8

Ingredients:

- 8 Salmons fillets, boneless
- A pinch of salt and black pepper
- Juice of 1 lime
- 2 Fennel bulbs sliced
- 4 Teaspoons olive oil
- 1 Teaspoon fennel seeds, crushed
- 2 Teaspoons rosemary, dried
- 2 Tablespoons cilantro, chopped

Procedure:

1. First, heat up a pan with the oil over medium-high heat, add the fennel and sauté for 2 minutes.
2. Then, add the fish and the rest of the ingredients, cook it for 6 minutes on each side, divide between plates and serve.

Homemade Turmeric Swiss Chard

Servings: 8

Preparation Time: 25 Minutes

Per Serving: 73 calories, 3.9g protein, 5.5g carbohydrates, 4.8g fat, 2.3g fiber, 0mg cholesterol, 247mg sodium, 493mg potassium

Ingredients:

- 2 Pounds swiss chard, chopped
- 6 Oz tofu, cubed
- 2 Teaspoons ground turmeric
- 4 Tablespoons lemon juice
- 2 Tablespoons lemon zest, grated
- 2 Teaspoons minced ginger
- 2 Tablespoons olive oil

Procedure:

1. First, in the mixing bowl, mix ground turmeric with lemon juice, lemon zest, minced ginger, and olive oil.
2. Then, add tofu and mix the mixture well. Leave tofu for 10 minutes.

3. Now, mix tofu mixture with Swiss chard.

Easy Roast with Turmeric Potatoes

Servings: 8

Preparation Time: 1 hour 10 Minutes

Per Serving: calories 290, fat 4, fiber 7, carbs 10, protein 17

Ingredients:

- 4 Pounds pork roast, sliced
- 4 Sweet potatoes, peeled and sliced
- 4 Tablespoons olive oil
- 2 Teaspoons rosemary, dried
- 2 Teaspoons turmeric powder
- 4 Yellow onions, sliced
- 1 Cup veggie stock
- A pinch of salt and black pepper

Procedure:

1. First, a roasting pan, combine the pork slices with the sweet potatoes, the onions and the other ingredients, toss and bake at 400 degrees F for 1 hour.
2. Then, divide everything between plates and serve.

Homemade Hot Chicken Wings

Servings: 8

Preparation Time: 1 Hour 10 Minutes

Per Serving: calories 274, fat 6, fiber 8, carbs 14, protein 12

Ingredients:

- 4 Pounds chicken wings, halved
- 4 Tablespoons maple syrup
- A pinch of sea salt and black pepper
- 2 Tablespoons apple cider vinegar
- 1 Tablespoon thyme, dried
- 1 Teaspoon chili powder

Procedure:

1. First, a roasting pan combine the chicken wings with the maple syrup and the other ingredients, toss and bake at 390 degrees F for 1 hour.
2. Then, divide the mix between plates and serve.

Quickly Shrimps and Pine Nuts

Servings: 8

Preparation Time: 15 Minutes

Per Serving: calories 271, fat 4, fiber 8, carbs 16, protein 8

Ingredients:

- 4 Teaspoons lime zest
- 1 Cup olive oil
- 4 Tablespoons lime juice
- 3 Tablespoons raw honey
- A pinch of salt and black pepper
- 2 Romaine lettuce head, torn
- 4 Cups halved strawberries
- 4 Cups breasts, grilled and sliced
- 2 Cups canned peas, drained and rinsed
- 1 Cup sliced red onion
- 2 Avocados, pitted, peeled and cubed

Procedure:

1. First, a bowl, mix the chicken with lime zest, lime juice, salt, pepper, lettuce, strawberries, peas, onion and avocado.
2. Then, the oil and the honey, toss and serve.

Delicious Chicken with Berries Salad

Servings: 8

Preparation Time: 10 Minutes

Per Serving: calories 271, fat 4, fiber 8, carbs 16, protein 8

Ingredients:

- 4 Teaspoons lime zest
- 1 Cup olive oil
- 6 Tablespoons lime juice
- 3 Tablespoons raw honey
- A pinch of salt and black pepper
- 2 Romaine lettuce head, torn
- 4 Cups halved strawberries
- 4 Chicken breasts, grilled and sliced
- 2 Cups canned peas, drained and rinsed
- 1 Cup sliced red onion
- 2 Avocados, pitted, peeled and cubed

Procedure:

1. First, in a bowl, mix the chicken with lime zest, lime juice, salt, pepper, lettuce, strawberries, peas, onion and avocado.
2. Then, the oil and the honey, toss and serve.

DESSERTS

Quickly Melon Sorbet

Servings: 8

Preparation Time: 45 Minutes

Per Serving: 88 calories, 1.7g protein, 13.6g carbohydrates, 3.9g fat, 1.7g fiber, 0mg cholesterol, 27mg sodium, 456mg potassium

Ingredients:

- 8 Cups melon, chopped
- 1 Cup coconut cream

Procedure:

1. First, blend the melon until smooth.
2. Then, mix the melon with coconut cream and pour the mixture into the plastic vessel.
3. In conclusion, freeze the sorbet for 40 minutes.
4. Now, blend the sorbet gently and put in the serving plates.

Homemade Lime Strawberry Mix

Servings: 8

Preparation Time: 30 Minutes

Per Serving: calories 220, fat 2, fiber 3, carbs 8, protein 2

Ingredients:

- 2 Pounds strawberries, halved
- 4 Tablespoons almonds, chopped
- 4 Tablespoons coconut oil, melted
- 4 Tablespoons lime juice
- 2 Teaspoons vanilla extract
- 2 Teaspoons honey

Procedure:

1. First, arrange the strawberries on a baking sheet lined with parchment paper,
2. Then, add the almonds and the other ingredients, toss and bake at 390 degrees F for 20 minutes.
3. Now, divide the strawberries mixture into bowls and serve.

Easy Lime Berries Mix

Servings: 8

Preparation Time: 10 Minutes

Per Serving: calories 217, fat 7, fiber 8, carbs 10, protein 8

Ingredients:

- 2 Cups blackberries
- 2 Cups blueberries
- 4 Teaspoons lime zest, grated
- 2 Teaspoons raw honey
- 1 Teaspoon vanilla extract
- 2 Cups almond milk

Procedure:

1. Firstly, in your blender, combine the berries with the lime zest and the other ingredients, pulse well, divide into bowls and serve.

Homemade Yogurt Pudding

Servings: 8

Preparation Time: 25 Minutes

Per Serving: 241 calories, 14.1g protein, 23.6g carbohydrates, 8.9g fat, 8.2g fiber, 11mg cholesterol, 132mg sodium, 538mg potassium

Ingredients:

- 6 Cups Plain yogurt
- 14 Teaspoons chia seeds
- 4 Oz raspberries

Procedure:

1. First, mix plain yogurt with chia seeds and leave for 15 minutes.
2. Then, transfer the pudding to the serving glasses and top with raspberries.

Quickly Tibetan Almond Candy

Servings: 24

Preparation Time: 30 Minutes

Per Serving: calories 211, fat 2, fiber 4, carbs 21, protein 7

Ingredients:

- 8 Ounces almond milk
- 12 Tablespoons lemon juice
- 1 Cup natural chicory root powder
- 1 Cup coconut butter
- 1 Cup coconut milk powder
- 1 Cup almond meal
- 1 Teaspoon ground cardamom
- 2 Cups almonds
- 1 Cup raisins

Procedure:

1. Firstly, in your food processor, mix the almond milk with lemon juice, chicory root, butter, milk powder, almond meal, cardamom, almonds and raisins.

2. Then, pulse well then spread on a lined baking sheet and place in the oven at 325 degrees F for 20 minutes.
3. Finally, allow the candies to cool down then cut into small cubes and serve.

Homemade Papaya and Nuts Salad

Servings: 8

Preparation Time: 5 Minutes

Per Serving: calories 140, fat 1, fiber 2, carbs 3, protein 5

Ingredients:

- 4 Apples, cored and cut into wedges
- 2 Cups papaya, roughly cubed
- 2 Teaspoons vanilla extract
- 4 Tablespoons almonds, chopped
- 2 Tablespoons walnuts, chopped
- 4 Tablespoons lemon juice

Procedure

1. First, in a bowl, combine the papaya with the apples and the other ingredients, toss, divide into smaller bowls and serve.

Easy Coconut Souffle

Servings: 8

Preparation Time: 20 Minutes

Per Serving: 269 calories, 2.3g protein, 8.8g carbohydrates, 26.6g fat, 5.2g fiber, 0mg cholesterol, 13mg sodium, 403mg potassium

Ingredients:

- 2 Cups coconut cream
- 2 Avocados, peeled, pitted, chopped
- 4 Tablespoons coconut shred
- 2 Tablespoons vanilla extract

Procedure:

1. First, blend the avocado until smooth.
2. Then, mix blended avocado with coconut cream.
3. Now, add coconut shred and vanilla extract. Stir the soufflé well.

Delicious Date Cheesecake

Servings: 8

Preparation Time: 2 hours

Per Serving: calories 220, fat 2, fiber 3, carbs 8, protein 2

Ingredients:

For the crust:

- 1 Cup pecans
- 1 Cup macadamia nuts
- 1 Cup walnuts

For the filling:

- 2 Cups date paste
- 4 Cups cashews, soaked for 3 hours
- 1 Cup almond milk
- 3 Cups strawberries
- 1 Cup coconut oil
- 1 Cup lime juice

Procedure:

1. Firstly, put macadamia nuts, walnuts, dates and pecans in your food processor and blend well.
2. Then, spreadinto a cake pan and press into the bottom of the pan.
3. Finally, pour cashews, strawberries, date paste, lime juice, almond milk and coconut oil in your food processor, blend very, thenspread over the crust.
4. Keep in the freezer for 2 hours, slice and serve.

Pineapple & Orange Smoothie

Servings: 2

Preparation Time: 10 minutes

Per Serving: calories 180, fat 1, fiber 6, carbs 14, protein 3

Ingredients:

- 1 tablespoon fresh grated ginger
- 1 teaspoon chia seeds
- 1 cup coconut water
- 1 orange, peeled
- 1 ½ cups pineapple chunks
- 1 teaspoon ground turmeric

Procedure:

1. Take your blender; mix the pineapple with the water, orange, ginger, chia and turmeric.
2. Pulse well, transfer to a glass and serve.

Bowl Heavenly Strawberry

Servings: 8

Preparation Time: 10 minutes

Per Serving: 51 calories, 1.1g protein, 12g carbohydrates, 0.5g fat, 4.2g fiber, 0mg cholesterol, 2mg sodium, 214mg potassium

Ingredients:

- 3 cups strawberries, frozen
- 2 teaspoons dried mint
- 2 cups raspberries

Procedure:

1. First, blend the strawberries until smooth.
2. Then mix the strawberry mixture with dried mint and raspberries.
3. Now transfer the dessert to the bowls.

Sweet Apple Compote

Servings: 8

Preparation Time: 30 minutes

Per Serving: calories 108, fat 1, fiber 2, carbs 4, protein 7

Ingredients:

- Juice of 2 limes
- 3 cups water
- 2 pounds apples, cored and cut into wedges
- 2 tablespoons honey

Procedure:

1. Take a pan, combine the apples with the lime juice and the other ingredients, toss, bring to a simmer and cook over medium heat for 20 minutes.
2. Then divide the mix into bowls and serve cold.

Pleasant Coconut Berries Mix

Servings: 8

Preparation Time: 25 minutes

Per Serving: calories 176, fat 4, fiber 2, carbs 7, protein 6

Ingredients:

- ¼ teaspoon vanilla extract
- 4 cups coconut milk
- 1/3 cup pure maple syrup
- 2 cups strawberries

Procedure:

1. Take a small pot, combine the coconut milk with the berries and the other ingredients, toss, cook over medium heat for 15 minutes, divide into bowls and serve cold.

Delicious Coconut Ice Cream

Servings: 8

Preparation Time: 8 hours

Per Serving: calories 200, fat 3, fiber 9, carbs 12, protein 7

Ingredients:

- 2 teaspoons vanilla extract
- 56 ounces coconut milk
- 4 tablespoons fresh grated ginger
- 1 teaspoon ground cinnamon
- 2 teaspoons ground cardamom
- 1/2 cup maple syrup
- 4 teaspoons ground turmeric

Procedure:

1. First, put the milk in a small pot, add ginger, maple syrup, turmeric, cinnamon, cardamom and vanilla.
2. Then stir, heat up over medium heat for 2 minutes, then transfer to a casserole dish. Spread and keep in the fridge for 5 hours.

3. Now transfer the ice cream to an ice cream machine and process for 30 minutes, then freeze for another 3 hours before serving.

Delicious Rhubarb Compote

Servings: 6

Preparation Time: 15 Minutes

Per Serving: calories 108, fat 1, fiber 2, carbs 4, protein 7

Ingredients:

- 1 Cup lemon juice
- 1 Zest of orange
- 3 Cups maple syrup
- 9 Cups rhubarbs cut into medium pieces.
- 3 Cups water

Procedure:

1. First, put the water in a pan add lemon juice, orange zest, maple syrup and rhubarb. Bring to a simmer over medium heat, cook for 5 minutes, then divide into bowls and serve.

Quickly Blueberries Sorbet

Servings: 12

Preparation Time: 50 Minutes

Per Serving64 calories, 0.7g protein, 16.1g carbohydrates, 0.3g fat, 2.4g fiber, 0mg cholesterol, 1mg sodium, 85mg potassium

Ingredients:

- 8 Cups blueberries
- 1 Cup apple juice
- 2 Teaspoons honey

Procedure:

1. First, blend the blueberries until smooth and mix the mixture with apple juice and honey.
2. Then, freeze the mixture until solid and then blend with the help of the food processor.

CPSIA information can be obtained
at www.ICGtesting.com
Printed in the USA
BVHW092351060521
606416BV00009BA/1030